Summary:

Made to Stick

By: Chip Heath & Dan Heath

Proudly Brought to you by:

READTREPRENEUR
—————— WORLD'S BEST BOOK SUMMARIES ——————

Text Copyright © Readtrepreneur

Legal & Disclaimer

damages, costs, and expenses, including any legal fees potentially resulting from the application of any of the information provided by this guide. This disclaimer applies to any damages or injury caused by the use and application, whether directly or indirectly, of any advice or information presented, whether for breach of contract, tort, negligence, personal injury, criminal intent, or under any other cause of action.

You agree to accept all risks of using the information presented inside this book. You need to consult a professional medical practitioner in order to ensure you are both able and healthy enough to participate in this program.

Table of Contents

The Book at a Glance

Every one of us has something to share. It may be fact or a life lesson. Whatever it is, you've deemed it important enough to share with the world. The problem, however, is that the world only listens to a select group of people who are able to weave messages that are ingrained in the minds of their audiences. So, how can you make your message "stick?"

Authors Chip and Dan Heath present their solution to this problem by emphasizing the creation of concrete, affective, and story-driven messages through a six-step SUCCES framework presented in this book.

• Simple: Simplifying a message means stripping it down until only the core message is left. What is difficult about stripping down a message to its bare essence is that it also involves the removal of details that are not as important as the core message. To make the core message stick, it should be applicable to daily life. Moreover, you can use "generative analogies" that relate your message to the practical experiences of your audiences.

• Unexpected: By presenting your core message in a new way, you disrupt the "patterns" that form in your audiences' minds, helping them focus on what you have to offer. After forming your core message, you should determine how to make your message stand out. You should then present your core message in a way that breaks from the conventional expectations your audiences may have regarding your message.

• Concrete. Messages stick because they appeal to the five basic human senses — these messages are concrete. Making your ideas concrete is the easiest of the six steps since it only involves associating your message with tangible things — concreteness is what helped Aesop's fables survive the test of time. Making your ideas concrete also prevents you from encountering the "Curse of Knowledge," where you are unable to share all your knowledge with your readers, instead giving them a vague message. Eliminating the Curse of Knowledge will make it easier for your message to "stick."

• Credible. Experts aren't always available to lend a helping hand when needed, so it is important that you establish your own credibility when presenting your message. There are five ways to gain credibility: first (and most commonly used), the use of an antiauthority who speaks on your behalf as an expert in the field your message tackles; second, a detailed knowledge about your topic, as people tend to believe more those who are well-informed; third, the inclusion of helpful statistics that strengthen your message; fourth, the passage of the Sinatra Test that recognizes you have enough experience to be an authority in your field; and fifth, the ability of your message to be tested by your audience for credibility (like the products advertised by Wendy's).

• Emotional. A great way to make your message stick is by including emotional appeal that can induce a stronger response; experiments show that people voluntarily donate more when their emotions are triggered. There are three ways to do this: first, by associating your message with something in which your audience is emotionally invested; second, by emphasizing how your message will benefit audience members by appealing to their self-interests, and finally, by emotionally appealing to the identities of your audience members.

- Story. Telling stories is considered the best way to make your message memorable. It is also the most effective method for eliminating the Curse of Knowledge. There are three very effective plot structures you can use: the challenge plot (overcoming obstacles), the connection plot (building bridges), and the creativity plot (discovering new things).

By implementing these steps, the authors conclude that a message can be remembered and appreciated by audiences for a very long time.

FREE BONUSES

P.S. Is it okay if we overdeliver?

Here at Readtrepreneur Publishing, we believe in overdelivering way beyond our reader's expectations. Is it okay if we overdeliver?

Here's the deal, we're going to give you an extremely condensed PDF summary of the book which you've just read and much more…

What's the catch? We need to trust you… You see, we want to overdeliver and in order for us to do that, we've to trust our reader to keep this bonus a secret to themselves? Why? Because we don't want people to be getting our exclusive PDF summaries even without buying our books itself. Unethical, right?

Ok. Are you ready?

Firstly, remember that your book is code: "**READ54**".

Next, visit this link: http://bit.ly/exclusivepdfs

Everything else will be self explanatory after you've visited: http://bit.ly/exclusivepdfs.

We hope you'll enjoy our free bonuses as much as we enjoyed preparing it for you!

Introduction

The book begins with an introduction to how certain stories tend to "stick" in our minds for some reason. Two ideas are juxtaposed: the kidney theft urban legend and a random quotation.

The introduction starts by describing the kidney theft urban legend: you're at a bar and a lady asks you if she can buy you a drink. You feel flattered and agree. The woman returns, handing you a drink, and you take a sip. At this point, you lose consciousness. You wake up in an ice-filled bathtub. After panicking for a moment, you notice a note instructing you to call 911. You do this, and the operator seems to be familiar with your situation because she asks you to confirm if there's a tube coming out from your lower back. She then informs you that your kidney has been illegally harvested.

This is an example of a classic urban legend that has been circulated for years. Which raises some important points. You have probably heard this story before — some facts may have been changed, but the basic details (the drink, the bathtub, and the stolen kidney) are all there. Second, it's told as the experience of "a friend of a friend," which suggests that it's an urban legend. Nevertheless, it's the kind of story that "sticks," something we remember even after hearing it only once.

This story is then contrasted with a random passage from a non-profit organization's paper that begins with "Comprehensive community building naturally lends itself to a return-on-investment rationale that can be modeled, drawing on existing practice," before going arguing that "[a] factor constraining the flow of resources to CCIs is that funders must often resort to targeting or categorical requirements in grant making to ensure accountability." It seems obvious that anybody would find it much easier to remember the urban legend than this excerpt. This comparison raises an interesting question: are ideas *born* interesting, or are they *made* interesting?

The introduction now turns to Art Silverman, a worker at the Center for Science in the Public Interest (CSPI), a non-profit organization that teaches people about health and nutrition. Silverman found that popcorn is an unhealthy snack that contains 37 grams of saturated fat per serving, an amount much higher than the recommended daily intake. The problem that Silverman now faces is how to communicate this information so that others can remember. Truth be told, "Popcorn contains 37 grams of saturated fat" isn't a catchy phrase and appeals to almost no one.

Silverman's solution was to "re-brand" the information and present it with visuals. The plan worked — the CSPI called a press conference, advertising a medium-sized popcorn in a typical movie theater as being more "artery-clogging" than "a bacon-and-eggs breakfast, a Big Mac and fries for lunch, and a steak dinner with all the trimmings— combined!" Along with this message, the CSPI also provided visual cues by juxtaposing these foods in front of the press.

The story was immediately picked up by top news channels in the United States, making newspaper headlines. Even members of the entertainment industry commented on and joked about the news.

This eventually resulted in people boycotting popcorn until its manufacturers removed the "bad" oil, forcing popcorn manufacturers to stop using coconut oil in their products.

This story teaches that a fact can be presented to be just as popular as an urban legend. The workers at CSPI knew that they had vital information that they should share with everyone, and they thought of an effective way to do so.

Let's examine the story and compare it to the urban legend. Of course, the popcorn story pales in comparison to the urban legend. There were no games of deceit, no bathtubs, and no theft involved. It was all about the fact that popcorn is unhealthy. In fact, the information is boring when examined in its bare essentials. The popcorn story is just like any other piece of information out there — it's boring, it's not interesting, it's not sensational, but it is *vital*.

People struggle to make ideas sound interesting, which brings us to the focal point of the book. The book is touted as a manual anybody can use to make their stories or speeches interesting enough to captivate and motivate audiences.

You may also need to consider why you want to make your ideas interesting. Out of all the possible things you can say, why should *this* particular fact be something that *should* be shared to the general public? This is the first question that needs to be answered to set your goal.

In addition, you should also be concerned about your target audience, as this will determine the success of your idea. What does your audience care about? What captures their attention?

The main problem with advertising messages and making those messages "stick" in the minds of your audience members is called the "Curse of Knowledge." Even though the presenter has a lot of insider information, much of this information is unknown to the audience. This can be illustrated by the game of tappers and listeners, wherein a person would try to "tap" a tune and have listeners guess the name of the tune being tapped. To the tapper, the game is quite easy, as he or she knows the song. However, the listener doesn't have this information, and has to guess the song based on the rhythm being tapped.

Based on their experiences, the authors have determined that there are six principles at play when creating a message that "sticks" in people's minds. These six principles will be discussed in detail throughout the course of the book.

Simplicity: The objective is to strip down your idea to its bare essentials. The problem here doesn't lie in removing unimportant parts of the message — the hardest thing to do is removing important information that is *not* essential. Therefore, the goal is to prioritize information. Which aspects of the message are absolutely necessary? Which are useful to the audience but not really important for them to know?

Unexpectedness: This idea has to do with capturing the attention of your audience. Rather, how can one maintain the eagerness of audience members to hear and share the information you impart to them? The best way to capture the attention of your audience members is to completely shake their expectations. Surprise and a continuous generation of curiosity and interest can help you engage your readers in a continuous discussion.

Concreteness: According to the authors, this is the easiest concept to implement and accept. An idea is considered to be "concrete" (and easy to remember) if it can be detected by our basic senses. This shows that the "Curse of Knowledge" is the worst enemy of an effective advertisement, since the former promotes the opposite of a concrete message.

Credibility: This factor focuses on the believability of the idea. As a person with an important message, how will you ensure that people believe what you have to say? A surgeon's ideas on medicine and medical technology will be easily accepted as fact. However, such an authority is not always readily available; doctors aren't always on call to verify the effectiveness of a particular medical product.

Emotions: Apart from showing concrete and simple facts to the audience, you also need to touch their hearts. Ideas need to have an affective aspect for them to "stick" in people's minds, as statistics and facts in and of themselves do not evoke emotion in people. Humans naturally gravitate to something concrete; they need to develop emotions towards a certain message for that message to be impactful.

Stories: Finally, a message should tell a story that encourages people to act on the ideas you share. Firefighters talk about their experiences with one another, helping each other develop job skills and knowledge that could come in handy in the future. In the same vein, hearing stories helps people respond to situations quicker and easier.

The authors explain that a person does not need to be a master advertiser to implement these principles. One simply needs to be compassionate and wise enough to understand what kind of information to share with others and how.

Chapter One: Simple

One of the most significant things you need to understand in order to make your message "stick" is to make your message as simple as possible.

The objective is to simplify your message by stripping it down to its core essentials. Weeding out unimportant ideas is the easy part. What's difficult is determining which of the remaining important ideas are *the most important*.

An example of finding the core message the Army's use of a Commander's Intent. The Commander's Intent, or CI, is a simple order given to military personnel that encapsulates both its goal and desired outcome. It is specific enough to be understood by its target audience but not too detailed to reveal any secrets. For instance, the CI might say "take the bridge" instead of providing instructions on how to take the bridge.

Like journalists, you should develop your message based on the "inverted pyramid" structure. The most important information is put on top of the pyramid and shared first with the audience, which is then followed by the second most important piece of information, and so forth, until the least important information is shared. This method is great since the message is directly expressed upon first contact. However, the issue with the inverted pyramid structure stems from the difficulties journalists experience in finding their core messages — what the readers really care about.

Any issues with finding the core and developing an effective lead can be resolved with the help of "forced prioritization." This means that as the writer, you need to force yourself to determine the most important information to be shared to the public. Say that you only have one shot at sharing the information you know — what would be the one sentence that entails everything you wish to say?

The problem with forced prioritization is that it can be very difficult, since one needs to remove all the important details except for those you are including in your core message.

You may think that it's not that big of a deal. From an outside perspective, it's easy to judge people for making wrong decisions when determining which idea is most important. However, step into their shoes and you'll realize that prioritization is more than just making a choice. This is because a message that "sticks" should include, above everything else, information that is "critical", followed by information that is "beneficial".

Distinguishing between what is critical and beneficial information can be a daunting task, especially since information can be *both* critical *and* beneficial.

This problem with choosing the most essential information can often lead to "decision paralysis", wherein you lose your actual ability to make a decision.

"Sharing the core" means using it to engage the audience in discussion. To motivate your audience members, you can let them apply your core message to make decisions.

The most significant part of this approach is to make your core profound and compact. That way, your message can imply a sense of urgency and worth that tells your audience to apply it in their lives.

A good way to create a profound and compact core is by pitching schema to your audience, which can be done by utilizing "generative analogy," an organizational framework that helps with idea creation. Generative analogy is especially prevalent in Hollywood; to obtain approval from studios to produce films, movie producers need to present "high concept pitches" that are essentially "core proverbs" in the form of analogies that help studios understand what the movie is about while also eliciting excitement.

For instance, the movie "Speed" was originally pitched as "*Die Hard* on a bus, while *Alien* was pitched as "Jaws on a spaceship." Moreover, *E.T.* was pitched as ""Lost alien befriends lonely boy to get home" while *Going on 30* was advertised as "*Big* for girls." What these phrases have in common is that they reference past movies and use simple words in order to explain the storyline of an entire movie.

Chapter Two: Unexpected

Now that you know how to create and identify your core message, the next thing that you should do is to get it across to your audience. One of the most important keys for effective communication is to capture the attention of your audience. You may not think that this is difficult, but given the fact that your message should "stick" in the minds of your readers long enough for them to understand and appreciate your message, it actually takes some work.

For example, consider how flight attendants give safety instructions to passengers. People don't usually pay attention to them (particularly those who fly all the time) because the safety instructions are all the same among regardless of which airline you're flying. This says a lot about your current predicament: important information is ignored because it is not conveyed in a manner that captures the attention of your audience. Although you can demand attention in certain occasions, many times you can't. What needs to happen is that you need to *attract* people so they want to listen to what you have to say.

The best way to be noticed is by bringing people something they don't expect. People tend to form patterns that help them to make sense of the world around them. If you manage to *break* these patterns, you create chaos and effectively gain the attention of your audience long enough for them to focus on you and your message.

However, note that humans can easily adapt to new patterns. Biologically, we find it easy to get used to continuous sensory stimulation, such as traffic noise, the hum of air conditioners, or the sight of something familiar (like a bookshelf in your home). People only become conscious of something if it is out of the ordinary. For example, if the air conditioner suddenly breaks down, it will catch your attention.

Apart from being able to adapt to new patterns, our brains are also wired to easily detect changes. Changes help capture the attention of humans. This chapter focuses on how to capture and maintain people's attention.

To do so, you must first understand two very important emotions: surprise and interest.

Surprise captures people's attention; surprising facts can easily captivate an audience. On the other hand, interest maintains people's attention. Different kinds of surprising things can continue to be interesting because they make the audience curious for more information. For instance, conspiracy theories continue to capture people's interest because new information and gossip about a particular topic is always being made available to fuel this obsession. For your message to "stick," it must be both surprising and interesting.

An issue with making things surprising is that gimmickry is difficult to avoid. It can be very easy to fill your message with gimmicks just to get the attention of your readers. Focusing too much on surprising people with gimmicks can take you off course, leading to a surprising yet confusing advertisement, rendering the element of surprise useless.

The best process to make ideas stick with your audience members includes the following steps:

- Determine your central message by looking for the "core." As discussed in the previous chapter, you need to determine what it is exactly that you want your audience to know.

- Understand what makes your message special. What information has the best chance of surprising your audience? Prioritize the most important piece of information and use that as a way to lure your audiences into discussion.

- Communicate your core message by surprising your audience. Do this in a way that will prevent them from relying on conventional guesswork, only for you to help refine it so they can understand your message.

- Add mystery stories to make your message surprising and interesting to your audience. Stories are a huge part of surprising people, as they do the exact opposite of informing — they keep audiences on edge, leading members to ask questions while keeping them on their toes.

- Open gaps in your message and then then gradually close those gaps. Studies have shown that audiences are smart enough to fill in the holes themselves. Therefore, it's your job to design your statements so that they first provide facts while withholding vital information that will not be easily guessed by your audiences before your big reveal. These "knowledge gaps" can help capture the interest of your audiences because the unresolved story has an air of mystery. Knowledge gaps pique your audience's curiosity to find out more about your message.

News reporters usually make ideas stick with their audiences by providing statements such as "a new drug is sweeping teenage communities today, and you may have it in your medicine cabinet. Stay tuned for more details." These statements sticks with audiences by creating insight and encouraging audiences to ask questions and expect answers. However, audiences are not entirely left in the dark because they are provided

17

with some facts; all they need is a few more details to piece the story together, which you will provide.

In conclusion, you need to find a way to make your core message unexpected for it to "stick" in the minds of your audiences. To do this, you must design your statement so that it interests your readers while leaving gaps to prolong their interest until you fill in those gaps. This way, you will encourage your audiences to communicate with you, making it easier for you to get your message across.

Chapter Three: Concrete

Another important factor that must be considered when creating a message that "sticks" is concreteness. Of the six things that you need to consider in order to create a sticking message, this is the easiest to implement and put into action. The reason why it is the easiest is because people natural gravitate towards tangible things.

Consider Aesop's fables, which have been famous for the past 2,500 years. Stories such as "The Boy Who Cried Wolf," "The Wolf in Sheep's Clothing," and "The Fox and the Grapes" are consistently popular throughout the centuries as examples of concreteness. These stories are considered concrete because they give readers a solid story that communicate a specific lesson. Now, compare the story of the fox and the grapes to a saying such as "don't be a jerk when you fail." Which one do you think will be remembered by generations to come? The story will undoubtedly be much more memorable for audiences, as the latter statement provided does not have staying power; it isn't memorable, just a fact.

Something is considered to be concrete when it can be detected by our basic senses. One of the best examples of applying concreteness is the mathematical education of children in Asian countries. Asian-educated children are generally more capable of solving mathematical problems compared to their American counterparts.

Many Americans assume that this is because Asian children are taught mathematics through rote memorization and rigid structures, but this is far from the truth. Researchers observed that some Asian math teachers would associate abstract numbers with real-life objects such as sticks and boxes to teach mathematical concepts such as subtraction. Not only did they learn mathematics with physical objects, but students also understood the concept of subtraction because they were physically "taking away" objects from a set of objects. An abstract idea such as mathematics was made concrete, making it much easier to learn.

This fact can also be applied in everyday situations. If you've ever read an academic paper, you may have been confused by unfamiliar terms in some works. Since you didn't understand the words, you may have wished that the authors could have provided examples to illustrate their points. Furthermore, when it comes to cooking, abstract instructions also don't make sense; "Cook until the mix reaches a hearty consistency" is much more difficult to understand than being told how many minutes to cook the mix or being shown an image of what a hearty consistency should look like.

When creating a message that sticks, concreteness should be prioritized. Human memory is designed to remember concrete words such as "avocado" or "bicycle" much more easily than abstract concepts like "personality" or "justice."

Other experiments have demonstrated the human need for concrete ideas. For instance, Jane Elliott, a third-grade teacher from Iowa, was faced with the difficult task of explaining racism to her students so they could understand why someone would want Martin Luther King Jr. dead. She devised a plan in which she divided the class between brown eyed and blue-eyed students, with the brown-eyed students being treated as the

21

"superior" group, getting perks that the blue-eyed students didn't get. This experiment resulted in the brown-eyed children feeling innately better than the blue-eyed children. On the other hand, the blue-eyed children felt that they were inferior to their brown-eyed counterparts. This illustration of racism resonated so strongly with her students that they still remember her classroom experiment fifteen years later on a television show. What this proves is that abstract concepts such as racism can be easily absorbed into the long-term memory if developed using concrete ideas.

Going back to the kidney theft urban legend that was discussed in the introduction, you will realize that this story sticks because of its many uses of concrete images. Notice that the basic "facts" of the story (the drink, the bathtub, and the missing kidney) are very notable, making the story memorable as a whole. Not to mention that there is a lot of available information about illegal kidney transplants.

The kidney theft story illustrates a significant point regarding the biggest enemy of concreteness called the

"Curse of Knowledge." The difference between a novice and an expert is that an expert can view things abstractly, while a novice only requires concrete evidence. This is true when contrasting a jury and a judge, wherein a jury relies on concrete images presented to them like people's clothing, mannerisms, and actions in the courtroom. On the other hand, the judge views these cases differently based on past experiences. As you can imagine, different views can result in different opinions even on the same case. The goal for you, therefore, is to speak in a language that everyone can understand regardless of their schema. This universal language will be the concrete concept you will use to get people to understand what you have to say.

Chapter Four: Credible

After concreteness comes credibility; you need your audience to trust what you're saying, and one way to gain people's trust is by establishing yourself as an authority in your field. We tend to base our beliefs on those of authorities, or anyone with enough skills or experiences. If we need to prove something, a professional can sometimes come in and verify things. However, this is not always possible. Therefore, how do *you* turn yourself into a figure of authority? This chapter deals with how you can make yourself an authority figure in your field.

There are five ways for you to become an authority: use an anti-authority, use concrete information, use statistics, use the Sinatra test, and use credentials that can be tested.

- Using an anti-authority: Imagine a scientist reporting that a particular bacterium causes ulcers. However, people don't believe him because they didn't understand the evidence he presented to support his statement. To prove his hypothesis, the doctor swallows the bacteria. He obviously developed ulcers, thus proving his statement and making himself an authority figure. Of course, you shouldn't have to swallow anything dangerous for you to make yourself an authority figure. An anti-authority can be used to demonstrate a point. A dying smoker can show the dangers of smoking, making that dying smoker an example of an anti-authority. Furthermore, a non-profit organization that claims to be helping homeless people find employment can send cars to pick up their clients, only for them to find out that the drivers are former homeless people.

- Using details: It's not always possible to get an anti-authority to vouch for your message. Therefore, as a speaker, you need to have "internal credibility." You need to be believed as an authority without needing to outsource credibility to anyone else. You can do this by having a deep knowledge of important details about your topic. For instance, custody was granted by a jury in a case where a lot of evidence was provided, regardless of how irrelevant the information is, compared to the provision of a few yet important details. Urban legends such as the kidney theft story and others also demonstrate that the staying power and authority of stories and people can come from their use of vivid details.

- Using statistics. Although this has countlessly been proven to be an effective course of action, it is still important to bear in mind that statistics need to be used correctly to work. Statistics don't have inherent meaningfulness — they are just numbers. Their ultimate purpose should be to show a relationship (or lack thereof) between two elements. It is much more important for your audience to remember *the relationship* rather than *the number*. Use the statistics as input, not as output; the statistics should be there to support your point, not the other way around. You can also ensure that your statistics are effective by making them more relatable; for example, you can use analogies and concrete examples that are easily understandable to your audience.

- Using the Sinatra Test: There is a line in Frank Sinatra's song "New York, New York" that should resonate with you: "if I can make it there, I can make it anywhere." In making yourself look credible to your audience, you can use the same mantra. An example is considered to have passed the Sinatra test if it alone can establish your credibility. For example, if you have For Knox's security contract, you will find yourself in the running for literally *any* security contract. If you've managed to cater in the White House, you will find it easy to compete for any catering contract. The authors use Safexpress as an example, which is a delivery company in India. Although it is popular with its "on time delivery", it has not yet succeeded in gaining the trust of Indian companies who were dubious of the high rates Safexpress charges. As a result, Safexpress decided to gain the trust of these companies by winning a delivery contract with a major Bollywood studio, a feat which was deemed implausible at the time given the prevalence of piracy in the country. However, since the company had experience in delivering risky materials perfectly — specifically the fifth *Harry Potter* novel which required the same, if not a higher level of security — Safexpress managed to secure the deal.

- Using testable credentials: You can make yourself and your core message even more credible by convincing your audience that they can test the idea for themselves. One of the most important example of this method is the "Where's the Beef" commercial advertised by Wendy's in the 1980s. The ad suggested that the hamburgers served at Wendy's contained more burger than bun compared to burgers from other fast food stores. Wendy's supported this statement by encouraging customers to verify this for themselves. Former U.S. President Ronald Reagan also used this tactic to win the 1980 presidential election when he asked "are you better off than you were four years ago?" during one of the presidential debates.

Making yourself a credible source of information goes beyond just knowing and having facts to support your statements. You need to have personal credibility through your knowledge of important details and experiences so that you are seen as a trustworthy authority by your audience members.

Chapter Five: Emotional

Once you've established your credibility, the next thing you should focus on is the emotional appeal of your message. As mentioned previously, people respond more strongly towards emotional appeals. However, this chapter will not focus on making your audience cry, encourage you to push their emotional buttons. That's actually a bit of an overstep. Rather, this chapter will focus on making people care about your message instead of being apathetic towards it.

In order for people to take action, they must care. The same principle extends to your message — if you want your readers to care about your message, they must be motivated enough by their emotions to do something about it.

To provide an illustration, the authors describe a study that showed the power of emotions to move people. This study was focused on the solicitation of funds for the starving children of Africa. The researchers presented two appeals — a carefully constructed appeal based on statistics and data, and an emotional depiction of one African child. The emotional appeal that used the child earned more donations than the one with the statistics; an interesting aspect of the study revealed that people tend to give more money each time they were presented with the emotional appeal, even if they were also shown statistics and data. However, donations severely decreased when participants were asked to focus on anything related to mathematics at any point during the conversation.

This study greatly demonstrates how humans can be emotionally motivated to act upon a cause while being unmotivated by facts alone. Putting on an "analytical hat" of some sort prevents people from feeling emotions, which in turn prevents them from caring about your message.

Therefore, your goal is to take off the analytical hats of your audience members. The best way to get your message across and acted upon is if you associate it with particular individuals. You can show how your ideas are 1) related to things that your audience cares about, or 2) appealing to their interests while also appealing to their present or even future identities.

The best way to make people care about your cause is to associate your cause with something in which they are emotionally invested. The power of association is an essential tool you can use to communicate your message to your readers.

The issue that you need to face is to find a novel way to associate your message with something your audience cares about. Though necessary, this can be quite difficult, as many words and concepts have been already used that they have lost their appeal, an issue known as "semantic stretch."

For instance, you may hear words or phrases that used to be popular; there are certain words that we deem as "lame" because they no longer appeal to us. Think back to the seventies when people used to say that something they liked was "groovy". Why exactly did this term go out of fashion? Probably because it was overused; the word "groovy" has been associated with being "cool" for so long that it basically stopped being "cool" itself.

This has happened very often with many words and phrases, so it's your job to find a new and interesting way to linguistically interest people in your project.

One good example of overcoming a tired phrase is the case of "sportsmanship." This word has lost its value and has become synonymous with "the prize given to the losers of the game." Since the word "sportsmanship" has lost its value, advocates decided that something should be done in order to get that value back. This was done by "rebranding" the word "sportsmanship" as "honoring the game", which gives people the idea that if they care about the sport, they will care about the game.

The same thing can be done with your message. Using the "power of association," how can you make your message stronger? What universally appealing idea can you use to emotionally petition audience members so that they care about your message?

Another idea that could help you get the interest of your readers is appealing to their self-interest. Advertisers can make mistakes by focusing on the features of their products rather than talking about their benefits, as customers can ask "Sure, this product has a lot of features, but how will I personally benefit from this?" Telling people that you offer the "best seeds" is weaker than saying that your seeds will give them "the best lawn in the neighborhood" which is really what your audience cares about.

People do not really talk about self-interest. However, this is one of the strongest appeals you can make that would make your audience care for your message. Advertisers don't talk about selling products by talking about self-interest, yet it's quite obvious that advertisements with the word "people" are more effective than those with the word "you".

When harnessing the self-interest of your members, you need to ask yourself the following questions:

- What will my audiences get from my message?

- How will they benefit from what I have to say?

- How will my core message benefit myself and my audiences?

Finally, you can also appeal to your audience emotions by identifying with them. Your audience don't simply agree to do something *just* because they will get something out of it. In a lot of instances, advertisers think that customers will buy products if the latter are given perks. However, what advertisers fail to realize is that customers make decisions not only based on things that they can touch, but also on their identities; customers often ask themselves who they are, what kind of situations they are in, and what people like them would do in the exact same situation. Intangible things such as a person's sense of duty and self-esteem play a pivotal role in helping people make their decisions.

This idea is demonstrated by a seller who was advertising his safety program to a local fire department. In his training, he was taught the three basic consumer appeals: sex, greed, and fear. He decided to use greed in order to get the fire department to get on board with using his educational films.

The advertiser originally got a resounding "yes" when he called the fire department staff and asked if they'd be willing to view the program he's offering. However, when he asked them whether they'd prefer a popcorn popper or a set of carving knives as a token of appreciation for reviewing the educational materials, the fire department staff took offense; they told the advertiser that they didn't consider to view the education materials just so they could get themselves popcorn poppers.

In the end, the most important thing to remember is that people need to be emotionally invested in your message to believe it. To emotionally appeal to your audience members, you can use three methods: using associations, appealing to members' self-interest, and appealing to members' identities. Regardless of which method you choose to use, the goal remains simple: get your audience to care about your core message.

Chapter Six: Stories

So far, the authors have pointed out very important rules when it comes to making your ideas "stick" in the minds of your audience — be specific with your message and present it in a way that surprises the audience to care about your message. The final thing you need to keep in mind to truly make your message impactful is by telling a story.

Stories are probably the most effective way to get your audience to not only communicate with you, but also to replicate your message in their own conversations. Stories stimulates the mind of audience members by cementing your message in their imagination so that they can remember it days or even weeks later.

In real life, this is always the case. For instance, it is much more effective to train pilots in flight simulators rather than using traditional teaching methods like flash cards or simple discussions. Teachers are encouraged to include the students' experiences in their discussion so that they would be able to remember the lesson much more effectively.

The difficulty in using a story to get a message across is that stories are difficult to create, especially if you're not the creative type. Fabricating stories from thin air may be hard, so an alternative would be to check your environment for available stories. You may not know it, but there many things around you that you can use. Many of the greatest stories ever told were discovered and collected, while only a few fabricated stories have ever stood the test of time.

The authors recount the story of a man named Jared, who lost 245 pounds by eating at a restaurant. Compare the effects of telling this story with that of presenting the company tagline "6 under 7, or six sandwiches with less than seven grams of fat." Between the two, the story is much more effective in inspiring people to eat at that restaurant. The authors also point out how Jared's story matches the criteria discussed by the authors to make a message stick.

- Simple: The core message of the story is simple — eat subs, lose weight.

- Unexpected: The story is about a man who ate himself slim. This story goes against our thoughts of fast food as fattening; since we consider fast food unhealthy, it is much easier to associate fast food with a fat rather than a slim Jared.

- Concrete: There are clear details — oversized pants, girth loss, and the subs. The story is so concrete it almost seems like one of Aesop's fables.

- Credible: The story is credible because it uses an anti-authority — a man who used to wear 60-inch pants has now reduced his weight and is giving us advice on diet and health.

- Emotional: The story focuses on Jared and his struggles. We know that the core message is losing weight, but the fact that the message was told through someone's experiences makes audiences care.

- Story: The story is about a protagonist who triumphs over his struggles; Jared's story inspires us to do the exact same thing.

By this, the authors prove that the best stories are discovered, not created. So, if you want your message to resonate with audiences, you need to find yourself a good story. According to the authors, there are three types of stories that you can consider using:

- Challenge Plot: This type of story would have your audiences rooting for the underdog. This is the rags-to-riches, triumph-over-obstacles kind of story. The key here is for the audience to see the character struggling against and finally overcoming obstacles. Case in point, Jared's inspiring weight loss.

- Connection Plot: This kind of story focuses on people who "build bridges" or develop relationships in spite of great differences. A good story will include friendships that transcend social status, race, religion, or demography. Connection plots are successful because they inspire the audience to connect with the characters. For example, the Mean Joe Greene commercial in the 1970s involved the titular character becoming friends with a small white kid. This kind of story inspires audience members to want to build their own relationships or to be tolerant of others. These stories teach love, compassion, and brotherhood in the face of overwhelming odds.

- Creativity Plot: This type of story focuses on someone solving a long-forgotten puzzle, making a mental breakthrough, or innovatively resolving a crisis. Think Isaac Newton discovering the laws of gravity by observing a falling apple. Such "eureka" moments are characteristic of a creativity plot. Another example is the cases of explorer Ernest Shackleton, who unified his men by keeping the complainers with him while the others were working, therefore minimizing the complainers' influence because they were isolated from the others.

By reviewing these story types, the authors are not intending for you to write your own stories. A story won't help you because you may not be writing or creating an advertisement. Rather, the goal is for you to learn how to spot stories in your environment that you can potentially use to make your core message resonate with your audience.

The use of stories also helps in eliminating the Curse of Knowledge. When stories are told, schema are activated. Stories can remind people of their past experiences, who then use those experiences to help themselves through their present situations.

Stories are great motivators. They are critical in getting your message out there because they actively demand the participation of your audience. Not only that, but they are also concrete, emotional, and are suspenseful. They are everything you need in order to get your message across.

However, the problem you may face is ensuring that your stories are simple enough for everybody to understand and easily remember. When searching for a story, think about what important and concrete details your audience needs to know. You should also think about the impact of your story on your audience.

Epilogue: What Sticks

This final part of the book recaps the main concepts that have been discussed. First, the authors posit the possibility of the audience understanding a different core message than the one you intended. For instance, Sherlock Holmes is remembered by many as having said "Elementary, my dear Watson," but in reality, he never really said those words. Ultimately, the authors judge that your effectiveness in sharing your core message to your readers not only lies in its ability to stick in their minds, but also in its ability to be properly absorbed by your audience.

For your idea to truly "stick," the authors believe that it should make your audience 1) pay attention to it, 2) understand it, 3) agree with it, 4) care for it, and 5) act on it. The framework discussed in the previous chapters simply elaborated on these areas.

It can be very easy to "guess" the effectiveness of the implemented strategies in making your ideas stick. However, it is difficult to verify whether your estimates are right or wrong. Consequently, it all depends on asking the right questions. You should be able to see that your readers can understand and care for your message. Not only that, you need to also be able to touch them with enough emotion so that your message will stick in their minds regardless of the time that passes.

The authors then talk about the strategies you need to take in order to implement the SUCCES framework effectively. The main strategy involves defeating barriers.

The first barrier you need to defeat is the Curse of Knowledge; you must first be able to share a core message that resonates with your readers. Second, you must eliminate decision paralysis by creating a strong message that leads your audience in the intended direction. Third, you need to eliminate the lack of knowledge a lot of your audiences will experience by sharing your core message so it is universally understood. Fourth, you should understand and remember these principles when developing your core message:

- Be concrete. Be specific with your intended message. Let it be simple and strong enough to be understood by a diverse audience.

- Have something unexpected in your message. Go beyond common sense. Make your message stick by telling it in a way that would garner the most attention.

- Tell stories. Attach your message to a good story that would be able to generate buzz. The moral is your message — find a story that fits it. An effective story encourages your readers to act.

With this, the book ends with well wishes from the authors, telling you to "fight sticky ideas with stickier ideas."

Conclusion

The goal of this book is to help you, the reader, find the best way to create a message that has a strong enough impact to "stick" in the minds of your audiences. The authors explain that there is a six-step framework you need to use in order to make this work. Your message needs to be simple, unexpected, concrete, credible, emotional, and story-structured.

• Simple: The most important thing to do in order to make your message stick is to focus on one specific "core message" which you want to share. Stripping down a message to its core means removing both superfluous information and important details. A great way to get core messages to stick is to associate them with the schema (experiences) of your audience by way of "generative analogies." Using these analogies to share your core message will make your idea popular and relatable.

• Unexpected: The goal in presenting your idea unconventionally is to create enough excitement among your audience members to pay attention. Humans tend to form patterns in their minds which assist them in cognition. Breaking of these patterns must happen for your ideas to attract attention. To do this, you must 1) determine your core message, 2) find the counterintuitive concept in your core message, and 3) design a way to present this message in the most surprising way possible without resorting to gimmicks.

• Concrete: The simplest way to make your message "sticky" is to ensure that it is concrete. For a message to be concrete, it must be something that can be understood using the five basic human senses. Stories such as Aesop's fables (particularly the story of the fox and the grapes) have stood the test of time because these fables have concrete elements that make them memorable to readers. Concreteness eliminates any misunderstanding caused by the Curse of Knowledge, and is thus a very important concept in making an effective message.

• Credible: Ethos is another important aspect in making your message "stick." The authors offer five ways in which you can make yourself look credible.

First, you can use an anti-authority as an authority figure who shares information relevant to your message. The problem with using an anti-authority is that it's not always possible to get one, so you need to build your own credibility — this is where the other four methods come in. The second way to gain credibility is having knowledge about your message to garner your audience's trust. Third, you can use statistics to support your message. Fourth, you need to pass the Sinatra Test, which means gaining an experience that grants you an unquestioned authority. Finally, you can gain the trust of your audience by having testable credentials. This means that you invite your readers to verify your message for themselves (like what advertisers do with their products).

• Emotional: An emotional appeal is also necessary in making your message stick. To do this, you can use three forms of emotional appeal. First, you can use the power of association by relating your message to a personal agenda that your audience shares. Second, you can also appeal to people's self-interests by describing how the message benefits them. Finally, you can also appeal to people's identities by clarifying how the message can help them personally.

• Story: The best way to make a message stick is by creating a story. Stories are ideal because they are concrete, have emotional appeal, and may have unexpected twists and turns. There are three popular plot structures you can choose from: the challenge plot, the connection plot, and the creativity plot.

FREE BONUSES

<u>P.S. Is it okay if we overdeliver?</u>

Here at Readtrepreneur Publishing, we believe in overdelivering way beyond our reader's expectations. Is it okay if we overdeliver?

Here's the deal, we're going to give you an extremely condensed PDF summary of the book which you've just read and much more…

What's the catch? We need to trust you… You see, we want to overdeliver and in order for us to do that, we've to trust our reader to keep this bonus a secret to themselves? Why? Because we don't want people to be getting our exclusive PDF summaries even without buying our books itself. Unethical, right?

Ok. Are you ready?

Firstly, remember that your book is code: "**READ54**".

Next, visit this link: <u>http://bit.ly/exclusivepdfs</u>

Everything else will be self explanatory after you've visited: <u>http://bit.ly/exclusivepdfs</u>.

We hope you'll enjoy our free bonuses as much as we enjoyed preparing it for you!

CPSIA information can be obtained
at www.ICGtesting.com
Printed in the USA
LVHW110826301019
635808LV00001B/24/P

9 781646 151530